FUNNY

▲▼▲▼

The Felix Pollak Prize in Poetry

THE UNIVERSITY OF
WISCONSIN PRESS
·POETRY SERIES·

Ronald Wallace, General Editor

Now We're Getting Somewhere · David Clewell
Henry Taylor, Judge, 1994

The Legend of Light · Bob Hicok
Carolyn Kizer, Judge, 1995

Fragments in Us: Recent and Earlier Poems · Dennis Trudell
Philip Levine, Judge, 1996

Don't Explain · Betsy Sholl
Rita Dove, Judge, 1997

Mrs. Dumpty · Chana Bloch
Donald Hall, Judge, 1998

Liver · Charles Harper Webb
Robert Bly, Judge, 1999

Ejo · Derick Burleson
Alicia Ostriker, Judge, 2000

Borrowed Dress · Cathy Colman
Mark Doty, Judge, 2001

Ripe · Roy Jacobstein
Edward Hirsch, Judge, 2002

The Year We Studied Women · Bruce Snider
Kelly Cherry, Judge, 2003

A Sail to Great Island · Alan Feldman
Carl Dennis, Judge, 2004

Funny · Jennifer Michael Hecht
Billy Collins, Judge, 2005

Funny

▲▼▲▼

Jennifer Michael Hecht

THE UNIVERSITY OF
WISCONSIN PRESS

The University of Wisconsin Press
1930 Monroe Street
Madison, Wisconsin 53711

www.wisc.edu/wisconsinpress/

3 Henrietta Street
London WC2E 8LU, England

Text and cover design by Mira Nenonen
Printed in the United States of America

Library of Congress Cataloging-in-Publication Data
Hecht, Jennifer Michael, 1965–
    Funny / Jennifer Michael Hecht.
        p. cm.—(The Felix Pollak prize in poetry)
    ISBN 0-299-21400-1 (cloth: alk. paper)—
    ISBN 0-299-21404-4 (pbk.: alk. paper)
    1. Humorous poetry, American. 2. Philosophy—Poetry.
    I. Title. II. Felix Pollak prize in poetry (Series)
PS3608.E285F86 2005
811'.6—dc22
                                        2005011174

For Maxwell

Our Yitzrock, "who laughs"

CONTENTS

ACKNOWLEDGMENTS

Thanks to the editors at the following publications, in which poems in this book first appeared.

American Poetry Journal: "Catch"

Barrow Street: "One End of an Orange Cat," "Song of Innocence and Experience," "The Sound of These Drums"

Black Warrior Review: "Family Life"

Conduit: "Funny Ha Ha," "Parrot in the Cold"

Courtland Review: "Hat Trick"

Gargoyle: "Horse Makes a Decision"

H_NGM_N: "Naked Man in the Window," "Betty," "Switch"

Harvard Divinity School Bulletin: "Cycling Down"

In Posse (www.webdelsol.com/InPosse/): "The Propagation of the Species"

Ms. Magazine: "Lifesavers"

National Poetry Review: "Cannibal Villanelle," "Three Boats, One Afternoon"

No Tell Motel (www.notellmotel.org): "Blind Love," "Gorilla in a Darkening Room," "Are You Not Glad?," "Sonnet on the Ribs of Laughter," "A Little Mumba"

Poetry: "Sonnet on Mirth," "Prosody on Comedy," "Fear of Flying," "Funny Strange," "Chicken Pig," "Story of My Life"

Verse Daily (www.versedaily.org/): "Catch"

Washington Square: "Love Explained"

The Best American Poetry 2005, ed. Paul Muldoon and David Lehman (New York: Scribners, 2005): "The Propagation of the Species."

"Gorilla in a Darkening Room" was nominated for a 2005 *Pushcart Prize*, by *No Tell Motel*.

Thanks to my husband, John Chaneski, for making me laugh and to our Max (whose Hebrew name, Yitzrock, "who laughs," was his great grandfather's) for the all the giggles. Thanks also to Amy Allison Hecht and Mary Elizabeth Keller who read whatever I send them, and fast, and so often give me the courage or advice I need. Thanks to the great people at the University of Wisconsin Press, especially Ron Wallace, Steve Salemson, Erin Holman, and Carla Aspelmeier. Thanks, too, to my friends and family, both funny strange and funny ha ha.

FUNNY

▲▼▲▼

Sonnet on Mirth

Of mirth the poets counsel little after
that present it be loved for present laughter.
Also that fool hearts, alone, let themselves belong in
the house of it; the wise, the house of mourning.
Why such divergent answers from such teachers?
Life seemed cruelly short to bard; cruelly long to preacher.
Yet true times run as rivers flow or candles burn,
long in the stretches, short on the turns,
and mirth with bitter herbs is better taken
than meals of mirth alone or years of it forsaken.
Does sweet improve when mixed with strain,
or is it that the acrid in that blend begins to fade?
Much endures while youth slips away like a thief;
mirth is a wine well pressed in the house of grief.

One End of an Orange Cat

Given the variables it's odd
that things narrow down one way
or another, but they do.
    Reminds me of the man
who had to knock on a door and tell
a woman he'd just run over her cat.
    That's awful, said the woman,
stepping out, as if to see it happen.
The man repeated an apology, said, *Please,
let me replace your cat. Well*, the woman
nodded, *How are you at catching mice?*

    The possible variations
seem excessive for the task at hand. Not only
for the story of your life, but also
for the universe as we have it, rather
than the myriad other possible universes.
In both cases, finally, the way
that it is, is
    the only way that it is. Infinite potential
options; one single one. Excessive
for the task at hand.
    Of course, he moved right in. That's
the violence of origins; the generative
splat of disaster. He fixes the roof,
hauls her ashes, but cannot find
much in the way of mice. Wonders,
sometimes, Why was this her
one condition?

    Life can't possibly have the time
to hand-pick all these minute exchanges,
so it must be narrative and need,
even narrative need, that creates
them, fills in the gaps, replaces
our murdered cats. A baseball game
or a day at the desk? Minute exchanges.

The answering of any question
is an attrition of possibilities.

   A replacement, a companion.
Sometimes he sussed the cat itself had been,
at one time, a sorry substitution
for a rotten love, now over
and listing toward forgotten.
   The story now becomes a comment
on her capacity for abstraction.
   The lost love had burnt-umber
hair, worked down by the docks. The cat
shows up one day in the woman's worst
despair, and who wants a cat? But then, she
sees his roughish orange hair; smells
fish breath; and there you have it: romance.
   By the time the cat is flat,
she'd loved it for its own array
of anecdote: the day it caught a mouse,
its extra toes, its appetite, its thick cat
hair on her goddamned clothes.
   The central tenant, companionship,
eludes her. In this, she is not unusual. When
looking for lovers, we often search for elements
of what we've grown used to. Ach
du.

   The man deliberates upon his actions.
Apparently, I killed this woman's cat.
It looked and smelled like orange roughy,
and I done crushed it flat.
   Now she loves me. I deserve that?
Yet she loves me, or says she does. It
would be nice if she could.
I will be vigilant
against the hated mice.
This life is mine.

Man knocks on a woman's door, one
afternoon in late September. Air smells of wet
leaves and weather. Woman nods, steps out,
firming a clutch on her sweater.

Each glances over and their eyelids
widen as if a wind had come upon
two butterflies and breathed their four
wings open to new notions.
Minute exchanges.

Hat Trick

A woman howling, her baby's bunk somehow
afloat in the river, taking on water. *Help,*
shrieks the mother. *Shriek,* helps the baby,
and a good man jumps into the river; splash

and paddle. Grabs the kid, hands the damp
bundle over. *Thank God,* cries the mother.
She cradles her daughter, looks up at the man,
says, *Excuse me, but she had a hat.*

The child grows up to be a hat-check girl,
always trying to get back what she'd lost,

always having to return it all by the end of the
night. She is often sorrowful and ashamed

for being sorrowful, surrounded by warm
coats, a stool to rest on while others,

elsewhere, spend all day bending. Wincing
anyway, she sharp regrets her bland

missteps, laments her ill use and fatigue. It is
awful: her feet hot with it, her head metal-cold.

You think it's enough to just keep
getting old? Can't I also have my hat?

Roots squeeze this information toward their
leaves: You cannot also have your hat.

After mother and child left, the man,
loitering the scene of his heroics

happened upon the little girl's cap.
Picked it up off the bank, startled by the tiny

scale of its protection, took it home, kept it
for years, then lost track of it.

It's been long seasons since he'd jump
in the sea like a fin in response to a splash.

To be so little thanked, so asked for more,
flattened in him what he hoped he had to give.

The mother grows less certain by degrees
that all that she had long awaited

had any sense outside the confines
of her blazing expectations.

The girl, fidgeting hairclip in cloak room,
her own self set by his one leap and her many

lurid resignations, braces waves of distress
and lets down her tresses. All three rail

their separate saga, he having labored
and netted so little; the elder she having

wanted so much from those around her
and found she was not so much let down

as skewed in her detailed attentions; the girl
wrestling a dreadful shadow: the facts

that throw us in the water in the first place
ruin us for much saving. She is aggrieved

of it, feels disgraced by the triumph of pain.
I want to comfort them, myself, my keen regret,

but am at best a lemon tree, vivid fruit
abundant among bleak green leaves. I will

wait for ice and sugar to be invented,
bees in the daytime, bats when it's done.

I will wait in the sun. I hope for relief like a
lunatic, indulge, like a drunk, in my croon.

It is my intention to offer lemonade while
there is time and so much brutal sunshine.

Meanwhile, I gather
hero and mother in my bower.

As for the girl, she's not a hat-checker
anymore. There's no such thing these

days. After an eon of servitude, men
stopped wearing hats, so she was free

to wander away from the 21 Club
and under my branches. Isn't she

beautiful? Didn't she have a hat?
To know, and arrange, and recover

even that. I am ridiculous, but it is
what is wanted.

Blind Love

Lady says, *Doc, I think I need glasses.*
Teller says, *You sure do, Lady, this is a bank.*

Lady wanders out, it's winter, wonders whether
other things have got mistaken, too.

At home she ambles through the house
with the sudden feeling that it all has been

rewritten. Notices a shadow as ivy peels from brick,
clatter of silverware drawer, a quarter

on her tiled bathroom floor. As on a vase the piper
plays not to the ear but to the more endeared

inner listener, so, quiet in an April afternoon,
late sun erupts a riot in her room.

Coin and cutlery glow red; wood glows golden in the hall.
Outside, ivy tendrils find new purchase on the wall.

Gorilla in a Darkening Room

A suspicion about oneself
in the midst of placid repetition
is a vehicle.

The suspicion is not a destination.

Obviously, the suspicion
should not be denied, but neither
should one believe it.

Let us imagine that life
in the arctic is going well for you,
though you are entirely alone
and the food is long gone; you've
made your meek adjustments.
The suspicion is a four-wheel-drive
all-terrain vehicle that appears,
with keys, one dark day. My point is:
it is important that you do not
simply begin living in the car.

Drive. Our concerns are the anxiety
of not knowing
where we're going,
and the terrific fear
of being given anything else to do,
of anything else appearing on our desk.
We tender resignation.
We succumb. We head back
inside and stick in a thumb.
It's a not uncommon, it's a common
error about how things get done.
How many gorillas does it take
to screw in a lightbulb? One,
but you need a lot of lightbulbs.

The gorilla regards
the crate of lightbulbs with excitement
but by noon, despair. My friends,
I admit, I cannot
bear the anxiety of not knowing.

Outside, the African sky bleeds blue
and oxidizes. Indoors, the one
light socket opens herself
to her gorilla and waits for the perfect
turn. Did you come here

to talk about love? Poor baboon.
This is no way to go about it,
of course, of course, we need
to be more honest, to admit
the secret weakness, the shattered,
well, let's move on.
You hear the socket coo:
My lonely gorilla, did they
punish you into perversion?

Under these circumstances
it is hard to be epic. The best
you can do is reopen the field
of possibilities and resist
rushing them closed. Bear
the anxiety of not knowing.
Resist summing up.
The secret weakness
wishes to speak! Nevertheless,
face it, nothing works.

It is winter in the African
jungle, and I am
empty. Below me, on the ground,
a silverback looks out
at the bruised-fruit sky of a setting
sun, then back up at me.

There's something about
fear of darkness in his attentions.
Crates of lightbulbs
everywhere and everywhere
broken glass. The terrible
graying gorilla is seriously trying
to figure it out now. He's

looking closer. I want him
to figure it out, much as,
in the other metaphor, I want to
park the car in the first town
I come to, buy a house, marry
the village wine steward,
and open a nice Chianti.

But you've got to roam.

The mango-papaya sky
at sunset in the jungle,
the aurora in the tundra.
Either way, be brave,
press the sky back into
the distance. Give yourself
a little room. Inside

the little room, dark now,
the gorilla sighs, the lightbulbs
sigh, the socket sleeps
and dreams about the rising
sun. So this is how the West was
won? This is how things get done.

The Sound of Those Drums

A man, walking alone
in the wild woods at twilight
begins to hear a rhythmic

pounding, resounding through
the space between massive
trunks of trees. *I don't like*

the sound of those drums,
he says, frightened, aloud.
There's a pause, then a woman

yells back, *He's not our regular
drummer.* Come out from in there.

Walk out from the darkness
between the evergreen and

deciduous and say it is ridiculous,
this hiding in my song. What

a bunch of brave beasts we
are; how talented it is

to fearfully play in our combo
even when we may be mistook

for threat of war, or, worse,
critiqued for our interpretation

of the score. How we arrive

with our casserole dishes
extended, our chocolate hearts

on a platter of fingers, lips
pursing in the plump of a kiss,

offered and offering! He takes her
in his arms, whispers that he is

always scared, she says she's
sensitive to negative critique.

He takes her in his arms, whispers,
I don't like the sound of those

drums, she says, *He's not our usual*
drummer. Through it all a sweet

groaning, intoning. The more
they understand of these

translations, the more
they lose interest in this plane

of existence. Instead, it is still
wintertime. People have been talking

a lot about snow. You are
letting go of even letting go. You are

listening, and it is sometimes
very interesting. You keep

your eyes at a faraway glaze,
You feel the weight of your hands.

The trees shimmer, tinseled
winter tremors in the wind. Things

have a salt haze. Life is a plump
plum today, a thump on your

skin, an unknown drum, humming.

Betty

Grasshopper goes into a bar,
orders a shot. Bartender says,
*You know, we've got a drink
named after you.* Grasshopper
says, *Ya got a drink named Betty?*

Yeah, we got a drink named Betty.

It isn't as much about her
as she was expecting.

Grasshopper learns it over and over
but can't seem to keep it
in my little green head.

Julep Hernandez visits Alabama,
her host says, *We got a drink
named after you.* She says, *Ya got
a drink named Julep Hernandez?*

Family Life

Old man lies dying, calls over his young son.
Says, *Son, come closer.* Son comes.
Son, says the dying, *My one last wish
is a piece of the crumb cake in the covered
cake dish downstairs.* Down goes the boy,
bounding and yessing. Five minutes later,
he's back and chagrined. Father says,
What happened? Son shrugs, *Ma says it's
for after.*

There is such a thing as group dynamics,
crowd behavior, synchronized
swimming. We want to bob alongside
the ornate bathing caps. We want
to snub Esther Williams and go off
on our own, but it's not as easy

as that. Everyone's got their gig
to play, but they're all scheduled for Ebbets
Field on the same day. That's why
it's so hard to find an audience.
Also, Ebbets Field was torn down
when the Brooklyn Dodgers broke

our fathers' hearts and left
for the West. Yes, two generations later
it's still a metaphor for betrayal,
but everyone feels the train tracks
for vibrations, then leaves town.

One way or another we all become

the other. How can the Brooklyn
Dodgers, then, be singled out for blame?

Old man lies dying, calls over his young son.
Says, *Son, come closer.* Son comes closer

like he's learned to do, leaning in for wisdom
like an ear to the track, backs away
from confrontation; still, swings when he's
up at bat. But every day more visible

become the needs he sees
around him instead of people, the placards
of distress, the more he does not want
to read them, or to want anything—thus to not
be them—or to join. Nevertheless,
the boy comes closer.

Downstairs, the memorial is already in progress
because people have come in from out
of town to see the old man down,
get a hotel room, iron their black cloth
and frown. People have begun looking
at one another and widening their eyes

as a symbol of the strangeness of the day
and its proceedings. On the lace tablecloth
sits a glass plate on a stand. Under its bell jar
rests a coffee cake. No one will eat it

while he is alive. Is it a matter of mis-
understanding? This woman, this wife
and mother, is downstairs. Not exactly
entertaining guests, but attempting to use

them in a way they are intended to be
used: to check them for reality, for in
reality this is how her life is going,
something might be gleaned from theirs.
She seeks to reconcile
the persistence of life in some, with
its imminent disappearance in the father
of her son. It's a tricky thought, and hard

to know, and knowing doesn't help. As
Groucho said, *Hello, I must be going.*

So when the boy asks about the cake,
may we hope she did not understand?
Perhaps the kid did not clearly say: *The old
man's last wish is on that cake plate. He is up there
beneath his own bell jar*

awaiting its moist goodness.
Perhaps he didn't and perhaps
he did. She might have
just said and felt, I need the coffee cake
that I baked for after,
to be eaten after. She might.

Most of us dream of our reunion more
before we've finished school than
after. After, after
all, we lose interest; the past passes, but prior
the vision of the later looms
paramount. There's nothing
we haven't imagined before it comes true.

As true as that is, it is not true, too.

So he is dead. I will sit. Preordained people
will mill. They will bring tea, and I
will eat a piece
of cake. Perhaps the kid will
have one too. Upstairs, the man will have blipped
out of existence,

his mummery of weird humanity, his list of ills,
his book of minor wit, his talent with a charcoal
briquette, will all fall out of the bumpy
present day. The man's tense
is going to change! My response will
be to cut that cake I made last night knowing
what I still know. *Hello, I must be going.*

Father sees the boy go—running and nodding,
coming up empty. It is a confusing
moment. The boy could not have

failed to carry out such a simple last wish.
The woman could not have denied
the dying man his coffee cake.
No one could insist that the coffee cake,
baked and set to get her through the first
moment, need be violated early,
the impromptu ritual ditched.

Or no one noticed any of this
happening at all. The man idly asked
his son for cake, not even knowing

it was there. He'd been asking

for a lot of things, even an egg cream,
a picture of the team that left town,
a cat that's been dead for a while. The boy
passed on this vague interest in cake
with his usual questioning solemnity.

The woman gathered some of what
he wanted. Kept the cake for after.

Or, in fact, she was getting him back
for some denial,
for this death or some other.

The group has a dynamic, it is swimming in
a pattern, and some days we do not think that
we can swim with it no more.

It is innocent, our failure
to divine the vital
heart, artery, and vein of these exchanges,
to answer each one's riddle
dead correctly, each
to each. But it is grievous,
all these fumblings.
There are so many mistakes.

By twilight, the 1957 Dodgers
are sitting shiva and eating crumb cake
in the suburban living room and we
have roamed from a simple question
of desires and how they go begging
into a dreamy kind of bullpen of the mind.
The lunkhead whose ill manner

sends us into monkish silence
to preserve our sense of sense
is sitting in the corner; it is twenty
years later. There is coffee cake
everywhere, crumbs on the tablecloth,
blue moon in the brave black sky.
Ma says it's for after. So am I.

Funny Ha Ha

Why this longing to speak? What good
could it do, to let you know that my
heart is a low note pressed from the bow
of a cello, like a church bell, like a failing
of the sky; a failing to hold back thunder,
a pressure against the quiet?
That's the ticket, cricket.
My magic sack of me, adorable self.
See you later, alligator.

You've heard the Borscht Belt time-zone
joke where if it's eleven p.m. in New York,
in Russia it's 1947? That's the sort of
category error I find myself up against
every day and it's not amenable to explanation.
In a while, crocodile.
For some reason, whispering these secrets
in your ear
has come to mean the world to me.

I have nuzzled in ersatz pastures and been wronged.
I have groaned on the prow of a boat and wanted.
That is why I turned to farm an Egypt of the arms.
Now we are free and drinking tea with milk and honey.

In the first week of 2000 CE, at the Oratory of Gallarus,
I took off all my clothes.

Say: Oh hell, pal o' mine,
better get back to the grave.
Say: Looking for a rally in a 9th-inning
groaner, driving pretty heavy toward the hoop.

Talent, footwork, charisma, he's got it all.
I have waited half a fiscal year for the pleasure

of your garrulous arrangement and I feel now
quite effectively redeemed.

This ever happen to you before?
No. First time? Yes.

Prosody on Comedy

Tragedy is when all the stage is all good will
and all will wrongly, like too many winter coats
in too few seats on the subway, no one will
give up a thing yet all feel a remote
and stinging sorrow for the standers. Still,
tragedy is the ship sunk, bobbing heads afloat
together in the drink, all happy now to fill
their lungs with air and dream of lifeboats.
No bouts now. All their coveted papers and pills
as wet as once were their eyes, dry as ghost's
now, and low slung. Comedy is why they're still
together, in an ocean wide as wind and sky her host.
As we float, the deepness of the ocean tugs our bones.
In comedy, we rush the crowded stage and act alone.

Horse Makes a Decision

Horse walks into a bar, orders a scotch.
Bartender says, *Hey, why the long face?*

It's who I am. Once I was coltish,
for a while I was a bit of a mare;

I cannot sit to the right of myself
at the bar; I cannot opt

to step over into something
else-ness. This is my long

strange moment of uncertainty,
that I can bend from what

I am.
This is the hangdog of doubt.

Horse walks into a bar, orders
a scotch whiskey, wishes she still

smoked cigarettes. For a while,
she muses, she was a bit

of a stallion. It's no longer
the central question.

Why the long
face? Well, why

the idiocy of
hope? The faith

that these plans of ours
come through

the way we want
them to, despite

the way things
generally go.

Born to brood?
No, not

the horse. Yet long-faced
with the weight of chin

and everything
else. I protest,

it is not just a matter
of learning to say Yes.

Or is it? The jaw jut,
the taut face,

downturned
corners of the lips,

mulling over even
the ability to choose.

Is this blind
groping choosing?

Horse walks
into a bar

orders a scotch and soda,
but gets a coca

cola, asks
for a do-over,

but it happens again
and again. Horse

is crying now,
bartender lending

his towel to it,
a drinking buddy

starts grooming her mane.
But there is nothing

for it. The simplicity
of it, the grace

of the question
is that she truly

has to answer it alone.
Horse goes into a bar in tap

shoes, does a few numbers.
Horse collapses

into the corner,
on comes the spotlight,

in comes the orchestra,
and suddenly she's singing us

her blues. Don't know why,
there's no

sun up in the sky.
Stormy weather.

Horse walks into a bar,
to get out of the rain,

to make a decision.
Bartender says, *Why*

don't you like Art Nouveau,
why do you want children,

why did you listen to so much
Dylan, what made you come

in here today, out of the sapphire
blue? Horse says, *I don't know,*

her jaw set low,
These are the constraints

of my nature. This

is my face. I confess,
I had hoped to be free.

Song of Innocence and Experience

Discovery we were hitherto naive
rarely informs us we are naive.

Instead, we are, once more, in the wise.

Two fools en route to a hunt
come to a fork in the forest road, sign
says, Bear Left, so off home go the fools.

How long this idiocy persists depends
upon the pressure need insists.

Headed home the hunters never make it there,
as each is stranded in the thicket of ill ease.

Furious with hunger, there with nothing,
the first one finds the wherewithal

to breathe. Stopped, the next one listens in intently,
but chokes on too much chatter in the eaves.

It is difficult to pitch one's ears precisely,
and eat only what one's eyes can bear receive.

So much thirst, yet so much clatter in the eaves.

The Propagation of the Species

It is likely that someone
will be standing there at the end
of time, looking up at the fireball
or down at the organs of desire.

It won't be us, but only because odds
are odds: uncanny, cranky, spare.
We may judge the world a safe
enough place. These are the cares
of the day, the age of probability
having replaced historic ne'er-do-wells
with numbers. As for us, we live in
surprise; why not share this mood
and facial disposition with some scion
of the future generation?

We spent our meditation-time instead
confessing. The exercise delivered
unexpected fruit. Perhaps we've better quarry
than the truth.

The fruit of all of this is
possession and release,
mango and bananas.

Especially bananas. Try expressing
to a friend, when next you are feeling
unglued or blue, say: *I'm bananas*. Explain
to others that your lover, while very
sweet and handsomely randy, is a mite *bananas;*
is bananas. With a meaningful look in your eye,

gesture an unpeeling.

It is your autobiography
you are living. The actor eating scampi
to my left says he is not yet off-book, but

will be. Folks, I am ever-so-slightly off-book;
Friends, I am bananas.

We parse the problem, nouning out the principal
players: friends, families, prospects. I interview
the possibility of a child;
ask it questions. Intone the word: *Interested?*
Then: *Want to learn the word for widget?*
Want to read Beowulf? Want to get named?

Shall we grin and bear it?
I admit, existence is where *woeful*
was conjured. Nonetheless, to recommend it,
there is Jell-O; average rainfall; the anchovy
app at Luna's; and the fact that in the middle, many
change their minds on the whole shebang—get
a good one off in both directions. But you and I
are going to have to choose.

It is our autobiography
we are eating; you snooze, you
lose. Still, in the midst of going too slowly,
all hell has been known to break loose.

A gang of snails attacks a tree sloth, steals her wallet.
Down at the station, police chief
questions: *How'd they get ya?*
Sloth says, *I dunno, it all happened so fast.*

Ain't it the truth. All this wallowing
in the details of engagement
and when the battle comes,
it isn't quite expected. It's slower. Also,
over much too fast to make a fair
assessment. Lounging in her tea tree,
chewing leaves and dreaming, she sees
them: wee, slimy things with spiral shells
and damp antennae that float like sea anemone
above their wet-tongue heads. She queries
softly: Is it a moment for decision?

Shall I bolt or battle? Or better yet,
might this pass me by without regret?
It took days for the battalion
to cross the stretch of trunk and reach
her, yet she was still in contemplation
when she found herself succumbed.
Years later, still on her way home
from the station, she wondered what
she had wanted with a wallet, anyway.

There is no way to parry ordinary disaster.
There are no odds worth playing.

Animal stars from early motion pictures
eat bonbons and wear feathered mules
in their trailers; the old-age home; the zoo.
What, on the other hand, will become
of you and I?

Side by side, the Studebakers inside us
ride along the Côte du Rhone,

our hair getting tangled in the violent wind of speed.

And how do you propose we un-knot
all these tangles? Not, I trust,
on the rocks below: brave souls pick
a hostel from the travel guide and go.

What do fools do? Don't know.
Probably the same but badly.
Bombardiers stay home. Bombardiers
are too aware of bombs to roam.

Still, it is a question of the result
of one's actions. Mendel, monkish,
watching pea pods, had a bright effect
on pillow talk in centuries to follow;
mumblings of the pregnant engineer.

What do you get from a threesome of a tiger,
a scorpion, and a fly?

Bumblebee.
How do you get a zebra? Mix a horse
and a tiger.
How you get a tiger? Mix a lion
with that same zebra from before.

Let us accept a rainy August day
as if it were a single, unlikely fabrication.
As if these movies had never been
 on television before, as if we'd never
heard of Mamie Eisenhower, as if her
bangs could still cause us to smile.

The recovering tree sloth hangs upside-down,
her three-toed feet hooked to the fat branch
above her as she lollingly observes
the tropic scene. *Much*, she muses,
to which we cling, turns out to be . . .
ah well. She's lost her train of thought,
chewing a mild leaf and swinging gently
with the breeze.

Odds of the home front; odds of the sun;
odds of a herringbone. Run, run, run.

Are You Not Glad?

Now that you have left
your black-hearted arrowsmith,

left his quiver,

now that you have, at long last, purchased him
a soft drink and punched him in the eye.

Now you are sane enough to stand my trials.
My dangerous vials. Knock knock.
Who's there?
Poison berries.
Poison berries who?
Knock knock. Who's there?
Poison berries. Poison berries who?
Knock knock, who's there? Orange.
Orange who?
Orange you glad I didn't say poison berries?

Orange you glad? No, I'm not. I ate the berries.
I was hungry; I was young.

Thrilled, yes, to have slept through the night,
got through the last wave. Slipped through my fingers.

See how my veins cling? But not much rocked

by the late arrival of oranges. Fie, fletcher.

Dangerous you, dangerous me. Surprises behind
every door, and all of them the same. Wretched

and fed on sun-ripened fruit. Spoiled for wealth
by famine, so much wanting when it counted.

Switch

What did the sadist do to the masochist?
Nothing.

To conquer is to let one's hunger overtake
the other ideas in one's head, to have dominion
is to flex and give pretense about the nature
of one's fixation, one must exaggerate
the situation. One generates
ideas.

To submit one has to wait for a thing to fit,
or click, or for the story that got you going
once to get repeated.
To take notes and parrot is delectable as a habit,
as is the repetition of a Sanskrit word,
but, face it,
what we are after
is a really good idea.

Being silent is thus a chore.

Then again, one begins
to yawn and grow curmudgeonly
when others write down what you say,
or when they fuss and act all conquered.
The drag is coming up with all
the words, filling in the time
when none but you may speak.

The world, when one is master, seems so
subdued as to give no true companionship

for one like you, a master. You plead
the room for an equal partner as you wield
your chin and groom your vicious hair.

Being conquered makes the world seem so
endless out in all directions while you are small
and central in your birdcage of a room.
You shut up; repeat what you're told.
For much of the day it may not get old.

Cannibal Villanelle

Two candid cannibals, stirring in some spice,
one says, I hate everyone. Says the friend:
Forget them now, you just eat the rice.

Well, of course, that all depends on just how nice
it tastes and if one is anemic in the end,
muse two uncanny cannibals, stirring in some spice.

I was a hermit once and may yet do it twice.
Interactions make me batso, but I cannot now pretend
to forget them, to eat nothing but the rice.

I wish these little gestures did not come at such a price.
The indigestion and regression is enough to send
any gentle cannibal off running for the spice.

Well, said one, perhaps just try a slice?
There have been great feasts, though we do tend
to forget them. Now you just eat. The rice,

I think, is only enough matter for a minor life.
If we want the meat, we must eat the world,
agreed two cunning cannibals, stirring in some spice.
Such meals are best in morsels with much rice.

Parrot in the Cold

We wing in on a westerly
to settle near the window of a tidy
moon-shone cabin, closer
to the sea than to the stars.

A glowing lampshade warms
the kitchen walls. When her foul-mouthed
father died he left to her his parrot.
It cussed so much she winced, insisting,

*I blame the old geezer, but if you keep it up,
I'll put you in the freezer.* Finally,
he overswore her mood to take it,
and with some vigor, in she tossed him.

Seconds later, she opens the great
white door with a finger, and marvels
at the wide-eyed bird she finds there.
So will you drop the vile profanity,

*thus stricken through
with fear?* Bird humbly swears
fidelity, then hollers: *Now, what
the heck did all the chickens do?*

By the fourth time she throws him in,
he hardly minds it. The chickens

in there with him come
and go but he has grown blind

to their awesome nakedness
and even, truth to tell, the cold.

Making of his wings a green
and red judicial robe, he paces

and explains: *You chickens*
cannot yet see what this means.

I assure you, we are here
to learn two quite

different things. Your lesson,
as I understand it, is that not all

freezing is punishment.
Some of it is just the silence

of the room. Parrot thinks a while
but cannot conjure up a lesson

for himself. He is aware he's prone
to cursing but cannot dream that this

could be the genuine complaint,
and so dismisses it in its entirety.

In fact, he never really hears her
asking him to quit. He thinks

her constant barking on his cursing
is an unimportant symptom of a much

more trenchant wound, and so,
ignores it. Puzzling all the while

why she throws him in there all
the time, both of them demanding

Why is my love so cruel? Once
alone again, a pair of frozen squab

twitch in the ice-box night. One says,
I do not want to grow to be

the advocate
of anything

worthy of a fight. The other
offers, *I will refine my speech*

with every intonation.
Let us leave them

in their little bungalow,
and deep refrigeration. Let us once

again be forest birds,
and sing our conversation.

Fear of Flying

Why did the chicken cross the road? When
in disgrace with fortune and men's eyes, to get
to the other side. But when she is feeling better,
she ambles lighter and for lesser causes. Sometimes
just to shift her feathers. You cannot really die
by cause of riding high, by cause of passing well
from one encounter to the next, from sign to sign.
Roll, red faced, like planets roll, fat in the dream
of time. You cannot die by cause of riding
high, though you may feel it. Why did the chicken
put feet to the street? To survive it. The road
is long, but it is not wide. You can live through it.

Even unwebbed toes tread the moat, we note,
and laugh on the other side.

Funny Strange

We are tender and our lives are sweet

and they are already over and we are
visiting them in some kind of endless
reprieve from oblivion, we are walking
around in them and after we shatter
with love for everything we settle in.

Thou tiger on television chowing,
thou very fact of dreams, thou majestical
roof fretted with golden fire. Thou wisdom
of the inner parts. Thou tintinnabulation.

Is it not sweet to hand over the ocean's
harvest in a single wave of fish? To bounce
a vineyard of grapes from one's apron
and into the mouth of the crowd? To scoop up
bread and offer up one's armful to the throng?
Let us live as if we were still among

the living; let our days be patterned after
theirs. Is it not marvelous to be forgetful?

Sonnet on the Ribs of Laughter

Those who find the sun in every sorrow
may yet cry thunderstorms when in their hiding.
Not rarely, who teaches hope can barely borrow
what it takes to make it through a day's colliding,
that is why they talk so much of hope. Tomorrow
and today are both a moment in aligning;
joke is that the hawk-heart is a swallow
by night. Who hears the music also hears the sighing.
By night who sees light, by day so sees the harrow,
but never ruled by sun nor star as law abiding,
no, the bilious cloud that knows of sorrow
comes at its whim, as does its twin: the dove arising.
Be kind to us we singers of delight,
we sing because we sigh in day and night.

A Little Mumba

In two billion years
the expanding sun will dry the oceans,
meanwhile, life has been around for more
than two billion years. Thus,
life on earth is at least half over.

There is not a lot of time
to get this figured.

Three geographers hike
an unknown South Sea Island,
raising minor mountains on their
field maps.

Suddenly they're pounced
on by a hidden tribe, grimacing
and wild. Brought before tribal
council, chief expounds
their choices: death or Mumba.

The first says, *I don't know Mumba,*
but death is bad.
So Mumba.

The crowd, elated,
yells *Mumba!*, throws geographer
into a pit and goes in after. Hours later,
out staggers the stranger, naked
and deeply rearranged. Does not
respond to any name.
Tribal council

asks the second: *Death or Mumba?*
Again, the answer comes Mumba; again,
crowd hip-checks the outsider, plunders in
after, voracious and obscene. Again, after
many hours, out crawls the map maker,
bedraggled, strained, and chewed.

Tribal council
asks a last time, *Death or Mumba?*
Geographer looks into the pit,
up at the stars, and says, *I want
to live, but I am not as strong as they.
I must choose death.* The crowd
is silent. *A wise decision,*
says the chieftain, *Death by Mumba.*

Right.

It is hard to get through
without resolving against human
interaction. What stings we feel
are ferocious, inadmissible,
unseemly. They linger and steam.
Thus the right-thinking runt
shuts them down, apes the machine.

But in the end, friends,
it's either Mumba or death by Mumba,
so Mumba's better.

But oh my life, the Mumba of it all.
The unyielding Mumbasity of life, of life
with others, in particular, oh my time.

What are you so frightened of?
Of what are you so frightened?

The universe, for instance, has
clusters of galaxies, we are not jealous
of *their* cliques: and these galaxies are
so big that they make the difference in size
between us and a fly, well, negligible.

The chatter has so little to do with anything
that is the matter.

You've got to figure: they planned this trip
together, the three geographers, Hinty, Luce,

and Spoon, since June, and now it's April
and they're on this island measuring
and counting, mapping and sleeping in a
canvas tent and out comes this thoroughly
other from the bushes. Then it's the bum's rush
to the tribal circle, wide-eyed terrified.

You hear yourself say, *Mumba doesn't sound
so bad*, and then you are lost to it,
drawn in, engaged in battle, though you hate
to wrangle, there you are.

A long time later, the onslaught abating,
your resistance subsides as they do; once
alone, you crawl in the powdery dirt
toward the lip of the pit. One of those

against whom you struggled
grips your elbow, lifts you over.
You hug the earth as vertigo hugs her
after a stint in the tower. From this supine state
you watch Spooner and Luciotta as one makes
the same choice you made,
and the other goes in for the other.
A fly goes by, in its minor role of *fly*.

There is a great deal of action, but you
are out of it now, not yet certain whether
you will live through this or die. You do not
know when anyone at home will notice
that your trip has gone awry. You think
of your front yard, all the effort of youth,
the apologies. Perhaps you die now,
all that work come to nothing,
come to Mumba on a mild night, alone.
You've got dirt in your mouth and on a whim,
instead of spitting, you stick out your tongue
and taste the soft, cool earth beneath you.
You roll yourself over;
stare up at the ten thousand stars.

Crushed between the galactic world
and all these subatomic particles
is so much emotion: anger, pity, relief
and this emotion, though emanating
from such an inconsequential thing
as you, is as large a total
as is the cosmos, and elemental
as electrostatic charge.

Neither black holes nor spider nets
await us. Other webs do, but we are not
the size of solitude either, so must
accept them. It is good to remember
that our troubles only obtain
on this median scale of play; elsewhere is
unaware of them. All, then, we've
ever needed is a minute change in scale.

One of the wild ones is a poet, whispers in your
supine ear to confess and to remind: *My love
has me lolling around a crater
on the moon, sucking wheat stalks.*
Your bruised heart overtakes your senses.

I don't know whether you want
to hear it or not, but the next night
everyone is dancing,
the babies and the crazies and the flies,
under the spangled, leaf-framed sky,
and you can't help it, you join in.
That's how good dancing is.

Three Boats, One Afternoon

I

It's a flood. The water is up to the first floor
windows, and most of the many are gone already.

At his second floor desk, the man protests calmly
that life will save him. Now he's on the roof

watching the water edge up the eaves, and a boat
goes by. Inside, mottled people hail him in.

He demurs, *Life will save me.* Then another
boat, and another, and all the time more water.

Finally, the tide overtakes his feet and his heart
and his nose. Dead now, and angry, the man

screams out at life, *How could you thus
betray me?* Life shows up, like God

in the book of Job; says, *I sent three boats.*

II

How many boats? It seemed like a fleet.
Years ago, when we'd likely die by thirty-five,

the first boat in the harbor must have been
an ideal ride, but now, for instance,

no one ever dies. There is always something
wrong with the equation, since, by turns, every

body dies. Also, there is the possibility of swimming.

III

At his second floor desk, the man protests calmly;
then he's on the roof, watching the water.

All right, fine, I'll get in your boat, says the man
this time, tamed by his last demise. Now he's wet

and shivering, bailing rain cups out of the keel.
His house, by now, is gone, no way to go back

to its sloping roof and drown on it now. He
imagines its thick backyard brambles,

its hyacinth, its capacity to soak up days
of rain. From this ludicrous predicament,

the boat being drowned from above, the bailing
man lets out a moan regarding the quality

of his choices. What can we now admit?
Commitment to a course of action,

perhaps two. Three boats? One afternoon.
Now he wonders whether he chose the right

boat and where they're going. Where will
he live? The simple fact of having saved himself

is blurred by the ongoing peril. Mottled
people in the other boats nod him in bypassing.

Somewhere in the expanse of water behind him
is the square half-acre that once was home.

At last, in the boat, rising rainwater overtakes
his feet and knees and nose. Once again,

as in the other version, down he goes.
The argument for one choice over

the other turns out to be the value of a daydream
dreamt in the course of his day-long lifeboat

ride. The dream was of himself bounding upon
the exploding yet foreboding clouds,

soothing them with his stride until they
were fair and pale again and turned to air.

Chicken Pig

It's like being lost
in the forest, hungry, with a
plump live chicken in your cradling
arms: you want to savage the bird,
but you also want the eggs.

You go weak on your legs.
What's worse, what you need
most is the companionship,
but you're too hungry to know that.
That is something you only know after
you've been lost a lot and always,

eventually, alit upon
your hen; consumed her
before you'd realized what
a friend she'd been, letting you
sleep in late on the forest floor
though she herself awoke
at the moment of dawn

and thought of long-lost
rooster voices quaking
the golden straw. She
looks over at you, sleeping,
and what can I tell you, she loves
you, but like a friend.

Eventually, when lost
in a forest with a friendly chicken
you make a point of emerging

from the woods together,
triumphant; her, fat with bugs,
you, lean with berries.

Still, while you yet wander,
you cannot resist telling her
your joke:

Guy sees a pig with three legs,
asks the farmer, *What gives?*
Farmer says, *That pig woke*
my family from a fire, got us all out.
Says the guy, *And lost the leg thereby?*
Nope, says the farmer,
Still had all four when he took
a bullet for me when I had
my little struggle with the law.
Guy nods, *So that's where*
he lost his paw? Farmer shakes
it off, says, *Nah, we fixed him up.*
A pause, guy says, *So how'd he lose*
the leg? Farmer says, *Well, hell,*
a pig like that
you don't eat all at once.

Chicken squints. Doesn't think
it's funny.

Love Explained

Guy calls the doctor, says the wife's
contractions are five minutes apart.
Doctor says, *Is this her first child?*
guy says, *No, it's her husband.*

I promise to try to remember who
I am. Wife gets up on one elbow,

says, I wanted to get married.
It seemed a fulfillment of some

several things, a thing to be done.
Even the diamond ring was some

thing like a quest, a thing they
set you out to get and how insane

the quest is; how you have to turn
it every way before you can even

think to seek it; this metaphysical
reframing is in fact the quest. Who'd

have guessed? She sighs, I like
the predictability of two, I like

my pleasures fully expected,
when the expectation of them

grows patterned in its steady
surprise. I've got my sweet

and tumble pat. Here on earth,
I like to count upon a thing

like that. Thus explained
the woman in contractions

to her lover holding on
the telephone for the doctor

to recover from this strange
conversational turn. You say

you're whom? It is a pleasure
to meet you. She rolls her

eyes, but he'd once asked her
Am I your first lover? and she'd
said, *Could be. Your face looks
familiar.* It's the same type of

generative error. The grammar
of the spoken word will flip, let alone

the written, until something new is
in us, and in our conversation.

Story of My Life

Each day goes down in history, wets its feet,
bathes in the clear or murky stream, drinks deep,
comes out to join past days on the other bank.

We go in with the bathing day, every morning,
brace the shiver on our skin, taste the slaking
of thirst, find footing on mossy rock. Climb out

with sleep. Waking, we're back on the first bank,
wading with a new day into the kaleidoscopic
water. Days far from either bank are barely seen

and seem unseeing. There is no recording of them
that knows the cold and quenching of their moment
in the water. Yet I cannot let them go, nor bear

the strong suggestion formed by their fading figures
that they have let us go and that those coming cannot
be foretold anything actual of water, flesh, or stone.

Publisher holds out a large envelope says, *Sorry.*
We can't publish your autobiography.
Man sighs, says, *Story of my life.*

All these words, then, are only for the stream?
The stream is everything? The stream is not enough?
The specters on the banks are deaf but listening?

Naked Man in the Window

Woman called the hotel manager,
said, *There's a naked man
in the room across!*
Tired and anyway never operatic
the manager came to her room already
calmly apologetic,
then looked out the window,
and wondered, *What's the problem?
You've only got upper
body from here.* He took some steps
over and added, *Here it's just shoulders
and head!* Said the woman, *Oh yeah?
Try standing on the bed.*

I surrender. The woman's heart is racing. She is
standing on the bed, projecting her face upward
with every midline sinew of her frame. *Buddy,
ya gotta see the view,* she said, winking
at the hotel's man, *This guy's a beaut.*

She says, *The world is a composite of shapes
and colors and they can all be taken on and off
the scene like some transferably adhesive
appliqué.*

Does she mean to imply
something about the reality
of the naked man? Has she
some sense that he could be peeled
off the background scene with three
fingers and placed like a tattoo,

on her arm,
his past location in perspective
having fixed him
several inches in size,
though still potent in his ability
to inspire?

The hotel manager looks up at her
unusual remark and sees the sun
glint set behind far buildings.

He looks her up and
down and doesn't
mind it; raises
his eyebrows to signal her
to brace herself for his ascent

and one hop later, he's up there with her,
looking out at the naked man, *Yes*,
he agrees, nodding, *The guy's a beaut.*

The manager looks around and, seeing
that she has swung closed the door, moves
closer to the woman. Muses, *So much was
hidden before I was reminded
of the motives of vision.*

Catch

One track befalls the lying artist:
his hand gets caught in a fact.

He grasps at last his rock of dying.

Hear about the trapeze artist?
Caught his wife in the act.

Latched her arms and found them flying.

Pressing onward is half based on slipping.
Even here tripping is better than rhyme.

It moves days on to other times.

Lifesavers

Off to the grocery, apple-red haired
Alice sees a sign for Madam Glib

the Parrot. For some reason, in she goes,
buys the bird, brings it home, then out again

to fuss her shopping. Comes back
to lime-green feathers on the floor and well

cooked carcass. Her sweetheart, June,
plum-yellow haired and sated,

greets her at the kitchen table. *Tell me
you didn't eat the bird!* screams Alice,

That was a talking parrot! June responds,
Well, why didn't it say anything?

At such moments, we will revert to
our most native language, our most

aboriginal form of conversation.
Likely as not Glib screamed her head off,

but in a parrot tongue unclear to June;
though surely the gist of the gesture

was unmistakably distress
as she read her: the hunger in the mirrors

of her eyes. Had Glib but muttered a phrase
of human patter, even of a wish to die,

she would have been retained at once.
Hungry June, we may assume,

would have found some other game for lunch
and nobly talked her through it.

But how is a bird to know for what
she will be cherished? Let's say it goes

the other way. June, raised on a farm,
very myopic and a tad peckish,

darts to catch and roast
the bird, but this time Mm. Glib says,

Whoa!, and June retreats completely,
offering her apologies and cups

of oat-brown seeds. Later,
the bird is alone on the back porch,

perching, looking at the stars. Wind
rustles even her delicate, sea-green

feathers, so that cool night air
touches the pale blue

parrot skin beneath. She turns
her face to it, so the breeze

blows right against her mind,
and wonders what they want her for,

these sweet yet frightening women;
red and yellow heads together drying

dishes in the kitchen window.
No part of me beyond my parroting

could justify my living? It is
good, concludes the bird, to be of use,
even without knowing what the use is,
and to be loved, despite all this misusage.

Cycling Down

Customs shack at a mountain pass. Every
week a woman peddling a bike
goes by and always with a bag of sand
slung in her cycle basket.

Customs man sifts with candor, but week
after week it's only sand. He gets to wonder.
One day he sees the woman and duty wavers,
blurts: *I swear I am no customs
man to you henceforth! Tell me
what on earth is going on.* Woman
says, *I'm smuggling bicycles.*

She rides away, almost standing, one long
leg extended, another poised. She comes
to a rough offshoot of the road. Dismounts,
walks the bike onward, then leaning it against
an elm goes on a ways without it, hauling
the sand on her back. Where is she going?
In deep. We catch glimpses of her up ahead
through the trees; we can see her hair
glimmer as it eddies around the dense bag
on her back and rides her shoulders. We
are a cloud of air chasing after.

Finally, we sense that she has come to rest,
and magnetically the space between us closes,
now we are in her hair, floating. She is sitting
in a clearing that is two feet heaped with sand,
dumping out her sack and groaning
with the work of it. We, the little cloud, seep

through her hair until we can see out of her eyes.
A tide comes up out of nowhere.
She takes off her clothes, and in we go, wriggling
among the finned.

They who swim forever know
the ocean does not end though it is finite.
The shape of it keeps you inside it.

At nightfall, a man comes for the bicycle.
We are not there to see it, but it happens.
The pearl-blue painted metal leans against
the bark, then its weight is shifted by a large,
hard hand; dry, yet still salted by a past
distress: walking past the customs house
he'd caught an unknown frown on that older
man's mug. Now it is dark and the cloud

that was ourselves is dissipated. The woman
is dry again; asleep between her sheets,
sprawling and curling in the slow pulse
of dreaming. The bicycle runner is gliding
on a near-dark road where mica in the asphalt
winks the moonlight. The customs man only
now packs up to leave his shack. He hears
final notes from a nightingale before
the engine of his faded car fulfills him
with its simple coming into being. It takes him
softly from the scene. The night is quiet.

AFTERWORD

An Essay on the Philosophy of Funny

The joke worries the ring on its finger, thinks itself over. Joke says to the psychiatrist, *It's no good if I have to explain myself.*

How I made up this joke: I wanted to write something about what jokes are; what it all meant. I'd broken each of the jokes like a coconut; planned now to drink the milk of it and offer what announcements seem bearable.

To begin, I wrote: *The joke smokes,* adding *its pipe* to distance myself from the gong of the rhyme, which I'd chimed for the dumb pleasure of it. This brought to mind a rolled-paper cartoon Joke, like the Bill from Schoolhouse Rock, but smoking a pipe, in an office. The joke is a shrink, thinking over a case. Whose case? Its own. So I threw Bill Joke on the leather divan and let Freud appear and assume the pipe and the chair while Joke offers his resistance: *It's no good.* I laughed. The gag combines something odd about jokes and something odd about psychotherapy: jokes work when shared knowledge, upon which the joke hinges, goes unspoken. Psychotherapy, by contrast, thrives on talk; the cure only happens when the secret links get spoken.[1]

The entire world of ideas may be split into two fields, the super complex and the super simple:

> Philosophy, physics, history, and biology are super complex. These disciplines make more explanations, systems, and ordered details than we meet in daily life.

> Paintings, poetry, Zen, dance, and jokes are super simple. These "arts of sudden knowledge" offer fewer explanations and systems than we meet in daily life.

Let me say that again, in another way: the science and philosophy disciplines try to make sense of everything through detailed, precise investigation. By contrast, what I am calling the arts of sudden knowledge don't concern themselves with making sense. These are appreciated when they succeed in snapping us out of our daily trance.

The sciences and philosophies count to ten by going up the ladder of numbers, the arts of sudden knowledge do not, instead they count to ten by contemplating "zero" and "one" so intensely that these figures show their hidden being, which includes the number ten. I just made that up, but I think it's good. Which is the quicker route to enlightenment? I don't know, but neither is easy.

Ideally, the complex and the simple meet at an unspeakably high place in a burst of sudden unified understanding of a vast, complex everything. That's ideally—it's been notoriously hard to check.

Jokes have the potential to tell us about how the world is unified, by grabbing opposing ends of something with one name; bringing the ends together so that what they have in common and what they have as difference becomes visible.

When I laughed at the Bill Joke image, part of what was funny was the pleasure I feel when I hear that someone has given up. The idea of giving up fascinates and tempts me. I laughed because when the joke sighs, *Forget it,* I suddenly give up too, and am glad to have someone express it. It's funny because of the grief.

There is a strong impulse to go on.

The arts of sudden knowledge are not about understanding the world through cataloging, explaining, and systemizing. Yet there are great books that catalog and explain the arts of sudden knowledge. Painting, poetry, and Zen have large areas in the bookstore. Theorizing about humor, though, is relatively thin. Jokes get short shelf.

Just as we may theorize the arts of sudden knowledge, the sciences and philosophies can reach heights of sudden knowledge. In the complex disciplines, what we really want is that kind of knowledge that must be true, in some sense, because everything fits together. Scientists long to be done with the details and finally get the big joke.

If we understood the world we would see connecting patterns throughout biology and physics, and between the two of them: consciousness, waving photons, a tired heart, and sharks; it would all fit together, from Uzbekistan to Andromeda, from the stew of culture, to the fact that the natural world lives by feasting on itself, all day, every day. Chewing on itself. The brain is meat and meat's got to eat. If we could hold it all in our minds for a moment, we would laugh. Jokes are one part suddenness and one part grief.

That's why jokes are the most important thing in the universe. Others before me have elevated silliness, nonsense, and absurdity to their proper place, but down they fall again, like a flock of sparrows that loves gamboling on the ground almost as much as foolish pomposity loves pretending it can fly over its own head.

The Ridiculous

Plato held that "the ridiculous" arises from lack of self-knowledge. People insist on the way they want to be seen, even though they know everyone can see them. In the Philebus, Plato has Socrates helping a student, Protarchus, understand the nature of the ridiculous.

> SOCRATES: The ridiculous is in short the specific name that is used to describe the vicious form of a certain habit; and of vice in general it is that kind which is most at variance with the inscription at Delphi.
> PROTARCHUS: You mean, Socrates, "Know thyself."
> SOCRATES: I do; and the opposite would be, "Know not thyself."
> PROTARCHUS: Certainly.[2]

Socrates later reveals that the "certain habit" mentioned above is when people think they are richer, better looking, or wiser than they really are. He adds that when powerful people do this, it is tragedy; when it's just people we know, it is ridiculous.

My version of this definition of the ridiculous is called *Great Red* and goes like this:

> A man comes to the town square in a blue suit and says, *Hello I'm Red-suit.*
> Everyone around him says *Hi Red-suit,* though some mutter, *Blue-suit.*
> When he leaves they say, *There went Blue-suit-who-calls-himself-Red,*
> while in his head he says, *Here I go, Dumb-ass Blue-suit-who-calls-himself-Red.*
> Or *Here I go, Great Red.*

Either way, it's funny. That comedy comes from people not knowing themselves seems evident once you think about it. Plato's notion adds humor to my Bill and Freud joke, since Bill may be said to both know himself (he is a joke after all, and his claim that he is better left unexplained is true) and also to not know himself (because he rejects entering the world of detailed efforts that obtaining knowledge about himself would require).

Plato also suggested that humor was based in feeling superior to someone. Two millennia later, the political theorist Thomas Hobbes said the same thing, with a new center of gravity: "Laughter is nothing else but a sudden glory arising from some sudden conception of some eminency in ourselves, by comparison with the infirmity of others, or with our own formerly."[3] This is the origin of calling laughter "sudden glory."

It is a vision of humor as mean spirited, but remember, neither Plato nor Hobbes thought much of most of us. Plato opposed democracy as mob rule, and Hobbes is best known for his claim that without authoritarian government the lives of most people would be "solitary, poor, nasty, brutish, and short."

Plato and Hobbes's idea on laughter is now called *superiority theory.*[4]

Superiority theory has champions today who claim that all jokes can be explained this way.[5] Most joke theorists don't find it sufficient because many jokes are derogatory, or at least exclusionary, but not all of them. The problem of what's funny floats higher than the thrill of the unkind: What's red and invisible?

No tomatoes. Kant explains in the *Critique of Judgment*: "Laughter is an affection arising from the sudden transformation of a strained expectation into nothing."[6]

No tomatoes. Orbs of fruit appear, then disappear. There are none, and they are red.

Comedy is a conflation of something and nothing. Schopenhauer, not surprisingly, takes this one step further: Laughter "always signifies the sudden apprehension of an incongruity between such a concept and the real object thought through it, and hence between what is abstract and perceptive."[7] Isn't that well said? Whenever we encounter things in the world, we understand them through concepts, and jokes happen with a sudden recognition of incongruity between a concept and the object thought through it.

Sudden and *suddenly* are remarkably oft-repeated words in the study of jokes. More than poetry is based on rhyming; laughter, of all human responses, is based on…timing. So part of every joke is about the conflation of concepts and things that results in expectations that burst into nothing. This part is dependent on brevity: the comprehension must be sudden or you "give away" the joke, and telling it now would be like trying to snap a wet twig.

The other arts of sudden knowledge often try to learn everything at once, but the attack doesn't work if it is too direct. Emily Dickinson put it best:

> Tell all the truth but tell it slant—
> Success in Circuit lies
> Too bright for our infirm Delight
> The Truth's superb surprise[8]

The timing of a joke gives it its absurdity, so I call it the *sudden* factor. The other factor, superiority, I call *grief*. The joke's mixed pleasure and grief is intense because when we laugh at others, we laugh out our own tension and misery.[9] Hobbes saw the importance of absurdity and surprise, but for him the fun was escape from the suffering on display.[10]

Good grief. There is a villain in humor, the rapier wit, the dark comedy, killing the room. I am further persuaded of this by Darwin's claim to the contrary.[11] Laughter, he asserted, is fundamentally the expression of happiness. For Darwin, children cry from pain, and it is still pain that makes us weep later (complicated pain) and is still happiness that leads to laughter (kids giggle at the arrival of chocolate cake, adults at complicated happiness of days and nights, together and alone). Maybe laughter does require some inner happiness. Still, think of two broken-hearted mourners at the end of a long day of grieving, suddenly making each other howl with laughter. That's not happiness, but it is quintessentially funny.

To step into the disjuncture provided by the joke, the strategy is to confront the suddenness and grief with ample time and empathy.

Power

Consider Proverbs 17:22: "A merry heart doeth good like a medicine: but a broken spirit drieth the bones."[12] Today we still speak of laughter as potentially curative, and we try to make sad friends get merry.[13]

Laughter can be a generator of happiness, a tool for manipulating one's mood. Herbert Spencer, a founding nineteenth-century social scientist, argued that the body is an energy system and when a situation produces more energy than needed, there has to be a release.[14] Freud developed this idea, arguing that because children have trouble managing their psychic experiences, they have to rely more on the body—thus the easy tears and bursts of laughter. We like laughing so much because it gives us back something we had before we got the joke.[15]

It can seem counterintuitive that laughter could so favor the world before wit. Children and fools laugh more than we do, though they don't get most of the jokes. It's one of the reasons the learned have been so suspicious of laughter. The complex doesn't get home faster than the simple. What could we have lost that was so conducive to laughter and so oblivious to wit? I guess simplicity and, with it, its secret ability to see unity and be at one with everything. Again, it is notoriously difficult to check on this claim.

Part of what we have bartered for our simplicity is participation in the shared social world. Early in the twentieth century, the French philosopher Henri Bergson wrote, "Our laughter is always the laughter of a group."[16] Bergson advised his reader to perform this thought experiment: You are at a restaurant and you overhear a group of people sharing stories and laughing. You might smile if something is unusually amusing, but you're unlikely to laugh. Bergson wrote that if you were with them you'd have laughed too, "but, as you were not, you had no desire whatever to do so." Laughter seems spontaneous, but for Bergson it "always implies a kind of secret preset alliance, or even complicity, with other laughers, real or imagined."

This collaborative part of laughter is powerful. It's warm for those on the inside of the group laughing, and it can be cold on the outside. Laughter is a water drip on the ice of oppression; the structure gets weakened and suddenly: avalanche. Politics may have to melt things a bit first, I'm not sure. But it does work.

Take Archie Bunker, for example. In the second half of the twentieth century, he was TV comedy's first outrageous bigot character. This guy was so clearly not better than the people he reviled, but he was human, and he didn't know himself very well. The program helped Americans talk about bias, class, race, and gender. Archie was also very protective of his chair. It was funny. Maybe you had to be there; in that particular moment of racial and gender tension: a guy protecting his throne against all comers, against any incursion on the vision he had of himself.

Laughter has uses as a local weapon, too. Classically, the seducer is prissy about his crime, and the girl begins to hurt his feelings with her black humor about it.

That's a lot of might for our lighthearted friend Laughter, and it doesn't end there. Absurdity is the plunge into being human despite the universe's insistence that we're kidding ourselves (because of time, death, and gravity). In art, absurdity often refers to existentialist theater, which actively practices ludicrousness, to strengthen its muscle. But absurdity has been around forever: a Zen master's tweak of the student's nose; the crazy images in the margins of illuminated medieval manuscripts. Shakespeare's fools were the wisest people around. To be humane in our context (where suffering will continue always) requires familiarity with absurdity.

Slow and Kind

I suggest two new centers of consideration. First: pity.

Which side of the chicken has got the most feathers? The outside.

What's a side, right? The joke produces a bare-skinned chicken with feathers on the inside. Again, I like the joke because I feel sorry for this inside-out chicken.

Another example: Two goldfish are in a tank. One says to the other, *Do you know how to drive this thing?*

I did not get this joke at first. I forgot about military tanks and guessed the fish thought the glass bowl was a vehicle. I found this sad and funny. In fact, I rewrite the joke: Two goldfish are swimming around as usual, and one says to the other, *Do you know how to drive this thing?* Poor fish does not yet know the fishbowl doesn't go anywhere.

Folks, this is a stationary fishbowl. I'm avoiding trying to discuss what I mean by pity.

What I mean by pity is that in order to open up the joke, I see now that I employed a technique of empathizing with individuals in the jokes.

Guy walks into a psychiatrist's office, he's got a duck on his head. Shrink says, *What can I do for you?* Duck says, *Get this guy off my ass.*

It is all just a matter of knowing with whom to have sympathy. Think of Hobbes's words, about being better than other people, and better than ourselves "formerly."

Laughter is also a marker of wisdom. In youth, you used to yell: *Hello, I'm Red-suit,* but now you let people see for themselves what you have got on, and maybe even the body within. Things that remind you of your past insistence on red cloth are funny.

So often do fools act alone that a test to know if you are being a fool is to see if you are acting alone. Not always—there are solitary heroes—but I wouldn't bet money that way. Maybe you think Abraham was wise with that close-call sacrifice of Isaac incident. I think he was nuts. Don't tell me your friend God told you to hurt that boy and then expect not to go into custody. That's cruel tragedy and its amazing friend drama, aka escape-from-tragedy. In comedy, the fool rushes into the public space and sets off on a course widely unrecommended, but there isn't too much awfulness to the error.

Busting Jokes

To get back to pity as a tool for busting open jokes: How is the trick done?[17] There is no slight of hand, just save someone. For instance: Put wheels on the fish tank and let the fish drive themselves around, exploring the earth like astronauts. You may find pity is hard to sustain. A new joke appears, wherein the poor creatures are forced to roam the world within their bowl, knowing people, but never really knowing them; watching the world go by. What's the joke? It's a cartoon. The fish are in an Italian piazza. A human hand shakes fish food into the bowl. They nibble and stare at the cafés all around them. One says, *It's exactly like France.*

It's funny because often people take what they believe with them wherever they go, so they never know there is anything else. I love a good refusal, but this is ridiculous. It's precisely as Plato defined the ridiculous. See, we are laughing at the fish and will have to go back and rededicate ourselves to approaching them with kindness.

The refusal to see oneself and others takes a lot of energy. People often know, "deep down," a few things that they pretend they do not know. The knowledge of what is really going on ghosts them like a stalker. They have to work hard to not notice it, lurking always in the corner of their scene.

Remember No tomatoes? At first your shirt is stretched to hold ten of them, plump in the bulk of life, hot from the sun. Then they are gone, your hands drop, your cotton shirt falls loose against your belly. The loss of them makes you take note that they had been real to you on several senses. The joke is a haunting.

The joke informs us that we had been thinking beyond the evidence, that our left brain has been spinning stories for us about what the incoming information is all about. With a nice snap of the context, the joke embarrasses the brain for getting so ahead of the sensory and intellectual information. You can't just keep announcing you are urbane, wise, selfless, or kind and think the rest of humanity will believe it.[18] They will make jokes.

Is this an issue of having a duck on my head or a person on my ass? And if I am the therapist, to whom do I send the bill? Say you agree to the duck's request to remove the guy, but then it turns out it's the guy who's paying? And what if he wants them to try to stay together?

So much is just a matter of learning to hold on and let go. As Elizabeth Bishop wrote:

> The art of losing isn't hard to master;
> So many things seem filled with the intent
> To be lost that their loss is no disaster.[19]

When Schopenhauer was talking about jokes, he mentioned asking someone: *What angle is formed by a circle and its tangent?* The person laughs because at the moment the circle meets a tangent, they are parallel and there is no angle, and yet there is an angle!

He saw the humor of geometry, and in so doing stated a geometry of humor. Mine is the humor of forensics and the forensics of humor. How do you know if an elephant has been in your fridge? Footprints in the butter.

There have been footprints in my butter. The elephant footprint leaves a complex pattern of ridges, as distinctive as a fingerprint, it's wide; bigger than the oval of my arms. What do you do when there are footprints in your butter? You become a detective. The size of the prints is what makes this just about the funniest joke in the world. Or, anyway, funnier than the one Schopenhauer told about the angle! That one stank up the room.

The inside of the refrigerator leaning back into the wall to accept the beast's advances. It requires a startling accommodation. Now the elephant enters, bends a foreleg and bows low its head; tips itself inward. I feel sympathy for the elephant, too, who doesn't come back from a joke like this; he just goes out the back of the refrigerator, never to be seen again. Is this a birth story, or a sex story, or an elephant joke? Why are there elephant jokes? Because they are so big, of course. What does it mean if you see nine elephants wearing blue tee-shirts? They're all on the same team.

I made up another new joke just now: Guy goes to the desert, says, *This place would be great if you could get some ocean here.*

The beach and the desert are such different places: one redolent with bodies, tanning oil and roaring waves, one barren with a solitude like outside Eden in any direction. Yet the difference between beach and desert is brief: they are both expanses of sand, the only difference is that one has an ocean.

Bill Joke says to Freud, *Dude, this place would be great if you could get some ocean in here.* Freud answers, *Herr Wilhelm, I totally agree.*

Also, we are laughing at ourselves, "formerly," as there was a time when, with all this sand, we thought the ocean couldn't be far. Before an arid grief made us grateful for rain.

In any case, there's something funny going on, and we will all make sense of it the best we can. For my part, I am slipping out the crevice in the joke, out the back of the fridge; the method is sustaining disjuncture. I am dragging out the sudden. I am drowning sudden glory in metered empathy. I will see all y'all later. I break the joke and then take the milk out and break that too. That's what I drink and recommend drinking. It's great if you don't have to explain yourself, but the only way to get to that place is by explaining yourself.

In this book, jokes have been forced to forgo their two primary features: suddenness and stinginess. If we slow down the joke a good deal and give more time and space to all its characters, what is left is disappointment, making do, and then happiness. The punch line isn't what you had prepared for, with all your narrative might; it is something else again, something, often enough, that goes by the same name.

The real world fails our expectations but frequently has pleasures greater than those we expected. Thus, the joke is the primary fractal of life; it is the emblem of the disappointment and I mean this in a grand sense: not only in the relationship of a concept to its thing, but in how things were supposed to be but never became, and then the surprising recovery into something new. We notice that this something new was there to be known all along.

Jokes are good for enlightenment, the generation of new ideas, escape from boredom, and as a vision of the progress of self-knowledge.

On our way from a life with cats to a life with love, we worry we'll be overrun by mice. At some point, we see that the presence of this love eclipses the mouse question. We feel we should have seen it for what it was at once, but at least when we look back, we can see it.

Notes

1. It was Anna O. who came up with the phrase; "She aptly described this procedure as 'a talking cure,' while she referred to it jokingly as 'chimney sweeping.'" Joseph Breuer and Sigmund Freud, *Studies on Hysteria*, trans. J. Strachey (New York: Avon Books, 1966), 29.
2. Plato, *Philebus*, trans. Benjamin Jowett (Oxford: Clarendon Press, 1953).
3. Thomas Hobbes, *The Elements of Law Natural and Politic* (London: Cass, 1969), 30–31. See also note 10.
4. Aristotle's take was sort of about laughing at other people, but for him it's more a matter of escape. Aristotle was said to have written a whole book on comedy, the *Poetics II*, but we have nothing of it. One of the few things he says about laughter that has survived is that it comes from "the joy we have in observing the fact that we cannot be hurt by the evil at which we are indignant." The danger is on the other side of the glass! Yet look what happened to Aristotle: we have none of his books, only lecture notes. Now that's comedy. You spend your life perfecting texts and then your students' and your own notes take you down through all proceeding history.
5. Laughter theorist Charles Gruner, for example, has claimed to be able to explain any joke or form of humor from a superiority perspective.
6. Immanuel Kant, *The Critique of Judgment*, trans. James Creed Meredith (Oxford: Clarendon, 1957), 201.
7. Arthur Schopenhauer, *The World as Will and Representation*, trans. E. F. J. Payne (New York: Dover, 1969), 2:91.
8. Emily Dickinson, "1129," in *Collected Poems* (Boston: Little, Brown, 1951), 506.
9. Plato is too good to miss on this. The following is from the same *Philebus* text from note 2 above:

   SOCRATES: Then the argument shows that when we laugh at the folly of our friends, pleasure, in mingling with envy, mingles with pain, for envy has been acknowledged by us to be mental pain, and laughter is pleasant; and so we envy and laugh at the same instant.
   PROTARCHUS: True.

SOCRATES: And the argument implies that there are combinations of pleasure and pain in lamentations, and in tragedy and comedy, not only on the stage, but on the greater stage of human life; and so in endless other cases.

PROTARCHUS: I do not see how any one can deny what you say, Socrates, however eager he may be to assert the opposite opinion.

10. Here is how Hobbes introduced his line about "sudden glory": "Also men laugh at jests, the wit whereof always consisteth in the elegant discovering and conveying to our minds some absurdity or another. And in this case also . . . laughter proceedeth from the sudden imagination of our own . . . eminence. . . . For when a jest is broken upon ourselves, or friends of whose dishonour we participate, we never laugh thereat." *The Elements of Law Natural and Politic*, 30.

11. Charles Darwin, *The Expression of the Emotions in Man and Animals* (New York: D. Appleton & Company, 1872): 196–219.

12. Psalm 51:17 has David, repenting of adultery and murder, plead, "The sacrifices of God are a broken spirit: a broken and a contrite heart, O God, Thou wilt not despise." So it is appropriate to break yourself down if you have made bad mistakes, but in general, it isn't healthy.

13. If you actually want to make people happy, it's best to work blue. As everyone's good friend the Roman philosopher Cicero said, "The chief, if not the only, objects of laughter are those sayings which remark upon and point out something unseemly in no unseemly manner." In other words, to make them howl in the aisles, act like you are talking about the sacred, but sneak in a mention of the profane. Cicero, *De Oratore*, E. W. Sutton and H. Rackham (Cambridge: Harvard University Press, 1996), 1: 372–73. Dirty jokes, that is, profanity, are another book. For now tickling the profane seemed mundane, so I dedicated myself to the mystery of the clean ones.

14. Herbert Spencer, "The Physiology of Laughter," first published in *Macmillan's Magazine* (March 1860).

15. Sigmund Freud, *Jokes and Their Relation to the Unconscious*, trans. James Strachey (New York: Norton, 1963), 236. Freud is marvelous on this. When we turn to comedy as adults: "The euphoria which we endeavor to reach by these means is nothing other than the mood of a period of life in which we were accustomed to deal with our psychical work in general with a small expenditure of energy—our childhood, when we were ignorant of the comic, incapable of jokes, and when we had no need of humor to make us feel happy in our life." The physical pleasure of laughing is so joyous because it has an aspect of semiconscious nostalgia.

16. Henri Bergson, *Laughter: An Essay on the Meaning of Comic*, trans. Cloudesley Brereton and Fred Rothwell (New York: Macmillan, 1913), 5.

17. I don't say *cracking* open jokes because of the importance of the phrase "cracking jokes," which refers to a whip snap (not a machete). I'll use *busting* to mean breaking them open.

18. Christian doctrine tended to be against laughter. Christendom, and monasteries in particular, frowned sternly upon laughing, following the teachings of John Chrysostom, Augustine of Hippo, Bernard of Clairvaux (all saints!).

19. Elizabeth Bishop, "One Art," in *Elizabeth Bishop: The Complete Poems 1927–1979* (New York: Farrar, Strauss and Giroux, 1984), 178.

NOTES ON THE POEMS

On "Sonnet on Mirth"

Ecclesiastes was written by Koheleth, often called "the Preacher," and
he suggests that misery tans a heart into the sort of leather we can use;
so despite the fact that he infused his version of sorrow with sardonic
humor, he claimed that in a long life, "sorrow is better than laughter."
Shakespeare seemed to counsel the opposite, that youth is a stuff that
will not endure, and so it had best enjoy itself today. By the way,
Ecclesiastes also says, "A feast is made for laughter, and wine maketh
merry: but money answereth all things." Everybody's a comedian.

On "Family Life"

The Groucho quotation is from the film "Animal Crackers" (1930), in
a song entitled "Hooray for Captain Spaulding," words and music by
Bert Kalmar and Harry Ruby (T. B. Harms and Co. 1928). The much-
awaited, famous Captain Spaulding has arrived at a high-society party
in his honor. This is a condensed version of his song:

SPAULDING (GROUCHO): Hello, I must be going,
   I cannot stay, I came to say, I must be going.
   I'm glad I came, but just the same I must be going.
   . . .
   I'll stay a week or two,
   I'll stay the summer through,
   But I am telling you,
   I must be going.
   . . .
ALL: Hooray for Captain Spaulding, The African explorer.
SPAULDING (GROUCHO): Did someone call me schnorrer?
ALL: Hooray, Hooray, Hooray.
JAMISON (ZEPPO): He went into the jungle, where all the monkeys
   throw nuts.
SPAULDING (GROUCHO): If I stay here I'll go nuts.
ALL: Hooray, Hooray, Hooray.